IMAGES OF AFRICA

In this work the internationally acclaimed author of
Langrishe Go Down (James Tait Black Memorial Prize-
winner, 1967 and Irish Academy of Letters Award-winner,
1970) adds a further dimension to his brilliant range of
fiction. In these diary notes Aidan Higgins conjures up
vividly and evocatively the different faces of South Africa
which he observed when he 'took the plunge over the
equator' in 1956. For two years he toured the country with
the John Wright Puppet Company and then spent the
remaining two years working first in a bookshop and then in
the scenario department of a commercial film company in
Johannesburg.

A writer's private thoughts - which are at once perceptive,
detached and compassionate - are set down here at
random to make a unique documentary. Individuals,
sketched in the briefest of phrases, explode into life. A
diary this may be but it has all the ingredients of a
stylistic masterpiece.

By the same author:

SIGNATURE SERIES

IMAGES OF AFRICA

Diary (1956-60)

Aidan Higgins

CALDER & BOYARS · LONDON

First published in Great Britain 1971 by
Calder and Boyars Ltd
18 Brewer Street London W1R 4AS

Parts of this material were published in French in:
Les Lettres Nouvelles No. 41, January 1964
Evergreen Review No. 24, December 1964
Transatlantic Review No. 29, Summer 1968

ISBN 0 7145 0774 1 Cloth edition
ISBN 0 7145 0775 X Paper edition

Printed in Great Britain by
Latimer Trend & Co Ltd
Whitstable, Kent

For JOHN WRIGHT
    puppet-master, traveller, driver, old friend

CONTENTS

PART ONE

'...I entered the wood; and, with all possible wariness and
silence, Friday following close at my heels, I marched till
I came to the skirt of the wood, on the side which was next
to them, only that one corner of the wood lay between me
and them. Here I called softly to Friday, and shewing him
a great tree which was just at the corner of the wood, I bade
him go to the tree, and bring me word if he could see there
plainly what they were doing. He did so, and came
immediately back to me, and told me they might be plainly
viewed there; that they were all about their fire, eating the
flesh of one of their prisoners, and that another lay bound
upon the sand, a little way from them, which, he said,
they would kill next, and which fired the very soul within
me. He told me it was not one of their nation, but one of
the bearded men he had told me of, that came to their country in the boat. I was filled with horror at the naming of the
white bearded man; and, going to the tree, I saw plainly by
my glass a white man, who lay upon the beach of the sea,
with his hands and his feet tied with flags, or things like
rushes, and that he was a European, and had clothes on'.

Daniel Defoe: The Life and Adventures of Robinson Crusoe

THE VOYAGE

I

The plunge over the equator. Flying fish sink, porpoises
rise, and evening after evening the sun goes down in
formations of cloud, furnace-like, dramatic as anything in
Dore's illustrations to Dante. The approaches to a new
continent. Such lovely leewardings! They must lead somewhere.

Undersized dining-room stewards, Malays, traverse
the decks banging out the same tune on their dinner gongs.
I've grown tired of the narrow regimen of shipboard life -
the repetitive meals, the same dull decks and the same dull
company - it's a kind of prison.

The passengers for the most part are Dutch or German,
or Afrikaners returning to their homeland. One tall
Afrikaner - von Lieres - is returning to Van Rhynsdorp in
the Cape after several years studying engineering in
Germany. He tells me that in some South African families
they send their sons into the police force for a year or so
to toughen them up before they take up a career. Before
they take up a more respectable career? I ask. He gives me
a blank look and smiles; we do not make jokes about the
police in South Africa. On the first lap of the tour we will
run into him again. I share a cabin with two young Germans -
also engineers. Going to German South-West Africa.
Strategists.

Among the German contingent there is a family from
Berlin. The parents sit close together on deck, stoutly
perspiring, handkerchiefs over their heads, calling for
beer. They have one son of fourteen; it's mainly on his
account that they are going to South Africa. Germany is
not for them anymore. Two wars in one lifetime - it's enough.

What is it they fear? Communism. Militant Communism.
The Tartar tank-crews with their slit eyes and Mongolian
features, their strange leather headgear of the Red Army

11

spear-heads that entered Budapest to crush the Hungarian
uprising, finished them. Emanations from a nightmare.
It is this they fear. Soviet tanks manned by Asiatic crews.

So off, then; pis aller!

The wife hopes to take up her old profession in
Johannesburg. Orthopaedics. The husband too will work.
Both have done so all their lives, worked hard, they are
not young anymore, but they will work for the future of
their son.

The small Fräulein in Jay's cabin has her wedding-
dress and trousseau with her. Though hardly more than a
child, she is going out to German South-West Africa to
marry a man she has never seen except in photographs.
She is a war-orphan from Hamburg. It's an arranged
match.

The first sight of Africa low on the horizon on the
port side, a dim white skeleton coast; a mirage that goes.

II

Walvis Bay, in South-West Africa. A barrage of heat.
Offal from the ship's kitchen floating astern. Seagulls
squall over it, their whiteness reflected in a rainbow trail
of oil. From the stagnant greenish waters of the roadstead
a stench of putrescence rises, sulphuric acid... rotten
eggs. A squat white bird resembling a penguin paddles
round the stern and one of the crew - an idle Malay - takes
pot-shots at it through one of the port-holes down by the
water-line.

Empty deck-chairs, inert in the heat, creak in the sun.
The wan looking bride-to-be is taken ashore on a tender
with some of the pale young Germans.

On shore, a collection of shacks face the sea, the sun
shooting fire off corrugated iron roofs. Die Waterman out
of Amsterdam, a decaying wharf with figures of African
dock labourers parading on it, and beyond them, an
excessively long rusty-plated terracotta Russian tanker
from the Bering Strait - on these the sun, from almost
directly overhead, brings to bear its fierce and implacable
rays. Baked littoral and saffron dunes, a reflection of a
decayed wharf swimming in mid-air, with figures walking
upside-down on it - all burn and tremble in the sun.

A local flat-boat comes alongside, and into its capacious and dirty hold black men dressed in rags, with bright-coloured bandannas about their heads, begin offloading cargo, while others wait down in the hold. The passengers, laughing, throw them apples and oranges, like into a bear-pit. The oranges explode down in the hold. Some of the remaining sallow-faced young Germans come with jackets under their arms to gape at the coal-black dockers. After a time the flat-boat sails, laden with cargo, grey-black smoke pumping out of its stack. That side of the ship now seems deserted. Leaning over the rail I imagine I can see sand, fathoms down. I see the reflections of a double-tier of bored passengers staring down. Their shadows go down shuddering into the deeper green of the sea, where a shoal of voracious red cannibal fish, like mullet, swim up out of the stench against our kelpy side. They come in dense, resolute shoals. When a fishing line, unbaited, touches the water they take it and one by one are pulled on deck. They lie twitching on the boards where one cannot walk bare-footed; quite soon their vivid colour goes.

This desolate place with its heat and smells, the hyena and lion reek of old Africa - this is Walvis Bay. Sidgewick, author of a beginner's book on astronomy, lived for a time with his girl in a cave up in the hills, and died later of heart thrombosis on a boat on the Seine.

At last this jaunt is nearly over. Tonight we lie to at Walvis Bay.

III

A storm before Capetown. All the ports bolted; the woodwork groaning. The Cape rollers begin. Black sea and waves at night. Nausea. We poor sailors turn in early.

In the morning, the storm has blown itself out, though the sea is still running high. We are into Table Bay, Die Waterman approaching its berth. A blinding glare comes off the sea. During the night one of the vague young Germans, wandering about the ship, fell down a companionway, suffered a heart-attack, died of it. He lies now in his white cabin. No one knows anything about him. He is to be buried in Capetown. A collection is started.

Provenance. Iphigenia.

Table Mountain looms over us, balancing on its summit a single cloud. It's a hot day in high summer here. The passengers crowd the rail. A beauty in a black dress, wearing sun-glasses, stands alone on the quayside and waves to someone standing beside me.

Prancing airs of the Cape of Good Hope. It's December 20th, 1956.

IV

On December 24th, two engines pull a long line of carriages through the Blaauwberg Mountains, on the Garden Route, travelling from Capetown to East London in the Eastern Province. Wheatlands go right up into the foothills of the mountains, which are lime blue. The horizon seems very far away, bright and luminous. Everything is on a grander scale here - even the swallows are bigger. At Mossel Bay, on an island, a lady in a picture hat paints at an easel.

Blossom, Le Roux, Zebra, Power, George, the Outeniqua Mountains, the beaches of Wilderness, the inland sea of Knysna, the thick green grass of the ostrich farms, an engineless grain train pulled into a siding and Africans in broken sun-hats unloading sugar cane.

On Xwartkops River, passing New Brighton location outside Port Elizabeth in the dusk of the evening. Lines and lines of hovels give way to arid land. An internment camp sprawls featureless in the evening dusk.

Nothing can be added and nothing can be taken away. An African shanty-town made up of line upon line of huts, hides and skins, open drains; through this lean cattle wander, mangy curs, ghosts. Most mournful aspect. Where the huts end the barren land begins again.

And in the twilight, clinging high on the wire fence like bats, naked piccaninnies stretch out their hands to the lighted carriage windows that are gliding slowly past, the dining-car passing; themselves the colour of dust, chanting: "Happy...happy...happy!" Happy Christmas in South Africa.

December 25th. I wake up. I am on the upper berth. The train has been stationary for hours, out on the veldt.

14

I feel warm air coming in through the carriage window and
all along the track the crickets are going like wildfire.
Then the long train begins to move again with much banging
and colliding of bumpers. Onward from Hex River,
Mossel Bay, Plettenberg Bay, to Port Elizabeth, East
London, King William's Town by the Amatola Mountains.

For a whole day now we have been travelling through this
landscape of grey-blue militant cactus with no other
vegetation, no house, the whole face of the land covered
with these things, and nothing else as far as the eye can
see, scarcely a blade of grass.

We pass an immense dam under construction in the back
of beyond, by the dusty shores of a lake. Africans in red
shirts, diminished to the size of flies, crawl on the dam-
face on scaffolding. We go round the lake. It's a beautiful
day. Someone is obliged to get out of the truck every mile
or so and open and shut gates, and all day long we pass
through this curious landscape.

As the sun is setting we come out onto a dust road that
leads to Uitenhage. The cars that pass leave behind them
a long wake of dust. Then we come upon this town built
upon an outcrop of little hills: Uitenhage. We've come from
Somerset East.

At the hotel we are booked in, some mail is waiting.
In our room the furniture reaches to the ceiling; the floor
shakes and there's a continuous roaring coming up from the
bar directly below us. It must be pay-day. We have a shower,
change, go down to dinner. We have Cape white wine - quite
good. Some of the company go to a film afterwards. I try
to read, but the roaring below is a distraction. It's like a
waterfall.

Next day we set up our marionette stage in the town
hall. Jay and I go for a walk. The streets are wide, the
buildings solid-looking, there are many Cape Malays; they
seem in an atmosphere of old and settled gentility - so it
must be a pretty remote spot, this Uitenhage.

The road runs out of town in a descending curve.
Coming up the hill are some Malays and their jaunting-
cars with big wheels and outsize hoods, coming in with
provisions; it's just like in the old colonial times here. We

pass one of these, its white hood and white wheels, driven
by an old man; he has a brown, wizened face, wears a white
linen suit and carries a long stick which he waves over the
mule's head. He salutes us - this is strange enough in
itself. We return his salute; out walking just like in the
olden days. He waves us on with his long whip.

I

We walk up to a plantation of orange trees to catch the
evening sun. It's outside a dusty dorp - name forgotten.
The ground is raked between the orange trees. We sit
there smoking and admiring the view. We see a stately
home far away between the orange trees. It's somewhere
in the Cape. Then we hear this thudding noise: something is
coming towards us. We get up in a hurry.

Forty yards off, going parallel to us, two ostriches
go jinking by, ruffling their feathers, spurning the ground
with their great prehistoric feet, their protuberant eyes
staring straight ahead.

II

The coldness of nights on the Karoo. Up on the chill plateau
lives an Afrikaans community, tight-fisted and suspicious.
It's another small dorp. Coming in, we pass two white
down-and-outs covered in dust, carbonized in appearance,
old, gravely saluting each other on Piet Retieffstraat;
Voortrekker stragglers.

A depressing hotel at world's end. Swing doors on the
bar like in the Wild West. The habitues look all the same -
tough, ugly, weather-beaten Afrikaans farmers, poor
farmers? share-croppers? Stench from the bar and the
bedrooms none too clean either. In the patio a lame,
injured tortoise drags itself into the grass.

Outside, in the white glare, a line of khaki trousers
belonging to Afrikaans police constables blows on a
clothesline. It's blowing all the time; the air shimmers. We
have poor houses. Loading the stage at night, after
midnight, it's freezing. Remote freezing night sky full of
stars. Is this the platteland at last?

Loxton. It's a town; it exists. The wind buffeting the

17

trees, and gross bulldogs on the ground. A town of bulldogs, surly brutes. A modern town hall - austere, Dutch
Reformed.

Over the verandah of the hotel there's a mattress with
a hole charred in the middle. The night before, a
commercial traveller, far gone in drink, fell asleep with
a lighted cigarette in his hand, and woke up with the bed on
fire. The others encounter him in the bar, his home from
home; blank stare and stout heart. A great imbiber of
good old Oude Meester brandy, man. He invites the whole
company, including the three charming girls, to be his
guests at a braaivleis after the show. It'll be late, after
midnight, for it takes more than an hour to bag the puppets,
dismantle and pack the stage.

So, after midnight, his African 'boys' cook meat for
the marionette company, with several fires burning on the
veldt, and plenty to drink; this is the life, man. When the
'boys' have finished cooking the meat he dismisses them,
'Get going, you buggers!' The poor buggers turn and begin
tramping away. It's a five mile hike back to town. Only after
an argument will he allow them to stay, take something to
eat. Going back, they stand on the running-board of his
car. Halfway back he stops, falls asleep over the wheel.
The day has been too much for him.

At seven next morning we are leaving Loxton again. I
look into his car; he's there, fast asleep and dead drunk
in the back of the car: the windows closed and his face
blackish purple, a dead cigarette between his fingers,
which were stained to the knuckles with nicotine. Rem-
brandts. Broken and mutilated creatures, best rendered
by their own debris.

III

The warm outdoor baths of... (name forgotten) Berkley
East? Skin of a dead lamb hung on barbed wire. (Where?)
The baths are thrown open at night for the London
marionette company. Pool and grotto and changing-rooms
constructed during the war by Italian POW's. It's mid-
winter, chilly, but the water is warm, greenish and
translucent under the electric light. Jane Tyson submerged.

Approaching Fort Beaufort in the cool of the evening,

we pass a line of young African bucks trotting by in the
dust of the road, all stark naked, daubed with white lime
from the crowns of their shaven heads to the toes of their
thick, misshapen feet; some carrying sticks, some with
burdensome erections: tattooed amakweta trotting by in the
cool of the evening, their childhood behind them.

News: Apostolic Brother commits nuisance with Bantu
girl in the bushes at Aliwal North, justly famous for its
healing therapeutic springs. Caught in the act, he denied
it all: 'I was singing hymns to myself and praying.'
Hymenal. Not acquitted.

Dutch Reformed Church domine (85) commits crimen
injuria with nubile African girl (25) under a car in a garage
in Berkley East. Not acquitted.

No one walks with impunity under palms.

The Institute for the Blind at Worcester. The blind
children working the machines. At the matinee, the
teachers tell them what's going on: 'Dit is 'n poppenspiel,
kinders.' Later, still as silent, dumb children sitting
under the trees as it's getting dark, knitting, reading
Braille.

IV

Report on Touws River. A freckled young woman with
brawny arms staring over a wall, looking for trouble.
What trouble can one create in Touws River? She's carrying
on with a stout, flushed fellow in a striped bush-ranger
shirt who stands on the near side of the wall (our side),
affecting indifference. She waves a carving knife playfully
at him. He has short-cropped fair hair; he stares off down
the road, over the bridge, where Bantus are walking into
town dressed in ochre-coloured blankets, carrying
provisions on their heads.

After a while he climbs the wall, drops down the other
side and suffers himself to be embraced. She stands behind
him with her arms about his neck. He stares down the road
at the approaching Bantus; a carving knife waves before his
eyes. 'Och, min, I kud drive it into yew! I ked cut yew!'

Valsh River and floods, vane and weathercock; intricate
silhouettes in sheet metal. The thin shagged spire of the

kerk rises over the hill.

Orange River: where the yellow weaver-birds build their cocoon nests in the branches of the willows that droop down over the water. Jay swimming naked across the river. The island.

A line of overburdened telegraph poles on the edge of the Kalahari Desert; every fourth or fifth pole weighed down with a nest as big as a haycock. The gregarious community birds.

V

A platteland scene: at Bramford, a small ill-lit dorp off the Golden Highway, in the neighbourhood of Bloemfontein. A rusty-bearded Ancient of Days sitting on the hotel step staring down at his hands and grimacing. Somewhere in the hotel women are imitating the high squealing of pigs. High-pitched shrieks of drunken laughter. Over the darkened houses, the lightning! Airlessness before a storm.

Deluges of rain. When it stops I go for a walk. Guitar music from some shacks in a field below the road. Africans coming down the hill from a location, out of sight. 'Do I know Jo'burg? I'll say I know Jo'burg!' African pride in the big city: the Big Time. 'Have you a drink for us, boss?'

I go back to the hotel for dinner. Two outsize waiters, 'Coloureds', overblown, like Mack Sennett villains, soft on their feet. Sucking pig on the menu; dinner for 5s. 6d. After dinner a thin lady carrying a Dutch Airlines grip accosts me in the hall: 'Are you by any chance a Roman Catholic priest?'

No, do I look like one? (scarcely) ... have I a dog-collar?

'Ah but sometimes they go without!' (this with a wistful look).

Outside it's pitch dark. No street lighting in Bramfort. I am tired of being in Bramfort.

Report: In an up-country high school with a roll-call of seventy girls (fourteen to eighteen years), five are pregnant. No one walks with impunity under palms.

A funeral on the coast. A small new Roman Catholic cemetery, the pall-bearers myopic old gentlemen, the undertaker a tall thin chap with pointed shoes, grey sponge-bag trousers and a frock coat, who goes like a dancer on his toes, his hands out from his sides, leading the cortege by a roundabout route to the grave-side. A box of rose petals handed out to the mourners. An inscription on stone.

VI

An eccentric couple on the coast: the Halishams. Madame Conny Halisham and Rodney, a retired bank manager, a sort of vague back-drop to the heavy drama. His wife, Conny, a famous singer in her day. She has a Jewish lover - a Chopin artiste, a remittance man, American. Rosen-bloom. He toured the colleges giving concerts. He came to the Halishams' house, was invited to stay nine weeks, but caught a cold and stayed twenty-five years. His dentures not properly in, pop eyes, 'boozed madly'. Madame Conny Halisham used to model in the nude on a stinkwood table while the lover, Rosenbloom, sketched her. Continually reproaching him: 'You don't love me any more. My body has deteriorated' (she is over sixty). He is getting on in years himself. She comes naked to answer the doorbell. The house is called 'As You Like It'. Coastal eccentricities.

The husband wears bloomers with a slit cut for the fly; pink celanese underwear. They have adjoining rooms in the hotel. He puts his feminine underwear in the wife's wash-basket; the maid holds it up and inquires whether she can mend the hole. On the beach the husband sits in a pool, Madame Conny fumbles about, trying to get one last stand; never successful. Continuous reproaches.

They keep pug dogs - these are 'all over the furniture'. A bitch confined in the middle of the night. The husband phones his friend Dr. Donnolly. 'I am not a vet, Halisham.' 'The poor dog is in great distress' (panting himself like a pekinese). 'Prepare yourself for tragic news, man.' Calling the doctor 'Dr. Jesus' when in favour; 'Dr. Shit' when out of favour.

Calling, calling.

21

VII

Coming from the Transkei, the vegetation changes all along the road, and by the time we reach the coast at Natal we have left the winter behind and it's summer again. Jay in the hospital at Pietermaritzburg being operated on for appenticitis.

The golf course at Pietermartizburg. The Indian pro. Subtropical flowers. The warm wind off the estuary and spongy grass underfoot.

2nd - 30th May, 1957. Phoenix Hotel, Moltino, Cape Province. This Foreign Legion outpost reminds me of Aran. The same famished hens, weary mistrustful peasants, the same high winds.

We toured the West Karoo for a dull month and are now creeping up the east coast towards Durban.

1st July, 1957. Marine Hotel, Port Shepstone, Natal. Here we are in Natal at last. A sort of third-rate Garden of Eden. Outside this room... paw-paw trees, orange and banana, wild palms. I can see the sea. Dull grey day.

We passed through the Transkei and East Griqualand on the way here. Astounding lands. Native Reserve Territory.

Our Afrikaans driver, Brink by name and brink by nature, has stomach ulcers but refuses to either diet or stop drinking. He was also instrumental in getting old Jospeh the African 'boy' sacked, and has added that pay onto his own. Brandy drinker. His eyes are bloodshot.

To date we have performed in just under 100 towns, one more or less like the other. A sky soggy as pasture is releasing rain. The sea disturbed, the palms waving, remote cars passing on the road to Margate, where we play tomorrow. Warner Beach next Friday, and then no more touring until 20th. It will be a relief to finish.

2nd September, 1957. Dixon's Hotel, Mafeking, Transvaal. In the past fortnight we have been as far north as Louis Trichardt, which is almost into Southern Rhodesia; as far east as Nelspruit, which is almost into Portuguese East Africa; and now as far west as Mafeking, the old siege town, which is within shouting, and shooting, distance of Bechuanaland.

Today is a public holiday. Settlers' Day. But not for this caravan. Jay is down with Asiatic Flu and appears to be dying. In one way or another we are all suffering from travel fatigue.

Dixon's Hotel was the GHQ in the famous siege. The tattered original flag is preserved behind glass in the Town Hall where we are to perform with puppets today. A dreary monument to the fallen stands in front, hard by the water-works. The plaque says: To the Memory of the Members of the Cape Boy Contingent... the Native Finco Contingent... the Black Watch... & the many Hundreds of Coloured and Native Non-Combatants who died by shot, shell and starvation, in Memoriam. Seige. King's Royal Rifles. And a roll-call of enlisted men who succumbed of wounds and diseases.

Today in the Town Hall, native servants, ill-paid and dejected, move about dusting the seats in a dream.

Outside, it's hot in the sun. Spring begins here.

Death is a silent picture, a dream of the eye; such vanishing shapes as the mirage shows.

Everywhere the peaceful face making way for the violent face. The actual terrain, too, violent. Violent colour, violent, combative contrasts, violent forms.

By November 30 we will have performed in 192 towns, and given over 400 performances... prior to Rhodesia.

Ansonia Hotel: the most pleasant of the entire tour - and we must have stayed in over 200 hotels. The tall good-looking receptionist in the sack dress with the haughty eye (just you try). A mock-Tudor lounge in the grounds; an annex with organ music. One Saturday night the resident organist dropped dead at the keyboard.

In the hotel grounds a lady guest in a red cardigan sits under the tall palm trees with a birdcage on her lap and stares at the canary. Stone tables like sundials are arranged informally; we sit there at peace, drinking gin. We are refitting and rehearsing a new programme in Natal University while the students are away. In the back of the auditorium I find two battered bowler hats, a tree with a single green leaf and some programmes - stage props for a past production of Godot.

The Notebooks of Malte Laurids Brigge in a second-hand bookshop, and a breast-feeding mother inquiring for

23

the latest Van der Post. The bookshop lady is very polite.
'And how is the milk, Mrs. So-and-so?' 'Oh eets jest
grained, thenks.' She improves the quality and quantity by
eating lots of peanuts and drinking lots of milk. Imbecile
cheerfulness of young parents.

A dead donkey on the roadside outside Durban; its
stiffened feet in the air, dried blood about the mouth and
anus. Guarded by another Neddy, standing there dejected
with downcast head. Fast-moving traffic into an industrial
town.

Small coloured flags, put there by Indians to ward off
evil spirits, in the high mango trees on the road into Durban.
Zululand, op!

VIII

A deserted beach that goes on and on. Shores of light. A
dolphin-torn, gong-tormented sea. Free of the others at
last we spend most of the day sun-bathing and swimming a
mile or so down the beach: Adam and Eve in the white dunes.
An Easter break at Keurbooms Rivier. Chalets. The sandy
path to the sea. Brink, our Afrikaans driver, is shacked up
with the local post-mistress's assistant and seldom appears.

One day in a clearing I come upon some Africans
breaking in a horse. A stallion. It rears up, rolling a
fearful reddened eye. A little brown man strikes fearlessly
at its head.

Wide-open eyes; bursting lungs.

IX

Travelling from Maseru to Ladysmith in the Orange Free
State, we come to the customs shed on the Basutoland
border early in the morning - five or six o'clock - and all in
a bad humour, cooped up together too long, suffocating with
heat and dust inside the National Theatre bus, which keeps
breaking down every second day or so. This ochre earth.
About to re-enter British territory, or a Protectorate, with
no flag flying from the mast.

Two African Customs men in Khaki uniforms; one sitting
on a chair outside the post having his hair clipped, his dusty
tufts. Flash of the scissors. The Union Jack wrapped about

24

his neck.

These are figures cut loose from a frieze; what you see of them - the little you can see of them - it's only a very small part of their existence; their existence in my eyes. It's nothing. These are unknowable shapes.

Under the feet of the oxen in a field or roosting in the low trees by the river, showing up as blobs of white against the dark masses of the leaves - tick-birds, the sacred white ibis; venerated in holy India, but not here.

THE RHODESIAS

Over Beit Bridge one breathes a different air: different and cheaper brands of cigarettes and spirits for sale beyond the Limpopo. - Bulawayo, Fort Victoria, Gwelo, Umtali, Salisbury, Blantrye, Kariba Dam, Livingstone, Victoria, Lusaka, Broken Hill, Ndola, the Copperbelt - all lie ahead of us. In Northern and Southern Rhodesia, and in Nyasaland, we will stay, whenever possible, in private houses, to defray hotel expenses, which are double that of the Union.

Here in Southern Rhodesia the settlers speak - not without ingeniousness - of the 'Yew Kai'. the good old Yew Kai, or United Kingdom, by which they mean 'home'. The Afrikaans settlers, on the other hand, do not speak of Holland as home, far from it.

Many of the Africans here suffer from bilharzia and are hardly fit to assist in unloading and then loading again late at night. They seem to have no energy, let alone gaiety. Bilharzia - it's a form of sleeping sickness; those who suffer from it are listless, rather emaciated, seldom smile, and urinate blood.

23rd February, 1958. Umtali, Southern Rhodesia. My teeth pain me, and the Rhodesian tour begins in floods of diarrhoea and torrents of rain. One listens under mosquito netting to the sting song of the skeeters. The nights are alive and warm, teeming with insects.

So. Delays by day at flooded rivers; sometimes a whole day goes by waiting for rivers to subside, and the schedule, in a few cases, goes awry. We go on. Wright drives us hard.

It's raining in Bulawayo. The rainy season drags on here, the rivers come down in flood, swamping the low-level bridges. It's a pleasant place with fancy homes set back among trees and ground-rents are high. Hillside, Bulawayo, an oasis. The McNairs.

Cigarettes are cheap. We buy boxes of 50 at a time.

26

Scotch 26s. a bottle. We are X-rayed, injected against
cholera, smallpox and yellow fever. The girls may go into
bars.

The low sky-line and wide streets, oxen carts going
through brown rainwater. A copy of A Portrait of the
Artist as a Young Man in Christian Vigne's bookshop.
Wide tree-lined streets of Bulawayo, skyscrapers of
Salisbury, and Africans so limp with bilharzia they can
hardly lift a load.

The suffocating heat of Wankie. Tintinabulation of
diamond-doves - cracking heat itself. Baboons in the
baobab tree outside the Baobab Hotel. Its air-cooled bar.

The native compound where we played on a cement
floor. Dire warnings posted up against venereal disease
behind us. The ruined homes in the crudely illustrated
warnings: Africans, Africans, beware of the pox!

Victoria Falls. We drive from Wankie after only a few
hours sleep. Walking in the rain forest. Livingstone.
African helpers weak with bilharzia.

Kariba. An Ethiopian-born Italian who can speak English
acts as translator. An Italian town built on African hills.
The Italian workers send seventy per cent of their wages
home, fraternise with African girls. Kariba Dam at night;
the partly completed dam walls. The blondins, operated
from towers, weigh fifteen tons, stand ten feet high and
cost £100 an hour to operate. When filled, the reservoir
will be sixteen or seventeen thousand feet deep and about as
wide as the Caribbean. No apartheid here. Lion tracks in the
fresh cement of the landing-strip.

Salisbury Hotel. A grey, wispy painting in the lounge,
a view of Victoria Falls, - made of porridge and pubic hair?
Hatfield. Drive-in cinemas vast as Roman amphitheatres.
The sky at night about Salisbury.

Curiosities: A battlemented 'Scottish' castle, turreted,
built of stone, a private lake, a swimming pool among the
rocks - a Union Jack flying over the castle. Owned by a
cattle baron, now in his sixties, with incipient jigs. He
drinks heavily; it's given him his dark mottled complexion,
his red, saltpetered cheeks, his gout, shaking hands; yet
he's a good host, if he cares to remember you. He started
out 'banging sleepers' on the railway; look at him now. He
buys and sells cattle to the Africans. We watch him setting

out on another auctioneering expedition, dressed in a
white linen suit, pith helmet, a monocle, riding boots,
ultra pukkah. His Memsahib looking like nothing on earth.
A luxury station wagon is loaded up with provisions for the
trip by a line of faithful black family retainers. Bwana
come; bwana go; bwana pretty damn rich. A kind of Gatsby.

Some of the company stayed in the castle. We had
dinner there when he was gone. It came up through the
service hatch. He has a good cook, and cellar. The
diningroom hangs out over the ravine with a view of the
lake. English hunting prints hang on the walls; a copy of
A Rebours (probably a mistake) among his nondescript
books. In the split-level lounge - a beautiful long room -
a Japanese officer's sword hangs in its scabbard on the
wall.

We go to a fancy-dress party at Salisbury. The long
avenue through Fortune's gate; the tenants' houses on the
estate are mansions. The architect's wife. Yashmak.
Wonderful eyes. She wouldn't take it off. A double-barrel
name, English; the cattle baron, safely returned, buying
rounds of Scotch. Drinking gimlets in the air-conditioned
bar; African waiters in scarlet tunics.

Tea-plantations of Rhodesia; acres and acres of tea-
bearing bushes. The rich Italian brothers. The ballroom in
their mansion set aside for the marionette show. Avarice
and prosperity beyond the Limpopo. The dead dog run over
outside the hotel at Umtali; the row of gaping Indian
children. The well-dressed crowd at the hotel door; an
elderly lady takes it upon herself to examine the corpse, the
bloodied roadway, dog's brains. The Indian children,
darkly beautiful, gape at her.

A generous tobacco farmer offers Jay a sixteen-foot
python skin, a twelve-inch hole blown in its head, as a
memento, for a handbag or a pair of shoes; she refuses.

The closed-in Copperbelt. A whiff here of the something ill; the neurosis of white Africa living and working
close to its wealth. Theatres and swimming pools for this
hard-drinking and soured community.

Lusaka; dinner with the abominable Pulsford. The
spirit's features stiffen into the social grin.

Mufilura, Northern Rhodesia. A copper mine. Italian
miners stuffing themselves with canteen food and drinking

chianti, their fat posteriors bulging over the chairs; in
the midst of adversity I am preserved.

Kitwe. Night on the road; the embankment of slag from
the blast furnaces. Tippers coming by rail all night long,
one every twelve minutes. The molten slag pouring down
into the darkness; two figures (African or white?) outlined
by the glare. Poured once, in error, on an African worker.

Blantyre, Zomba, Tet. Portuguese imported white
wine in Tet. Arab dhows tacking across the fast-flowing
Zambesi. Arrival in the evening. The ill-natured monkey
chained to its perch in the yard; yet a feeling of Europe
here.

One last image: Dedza valley in Nyasaland. The long
straight dust road through the pine forest. Grey, granite
highlands, and a damp mist coming down over the hills.
Relief at last from the perpetual heat and sweating.
Drinking tinned Watney's and Scotch. A green secluded
valley.

From the Cape to Kitwe, via Basutuland, Nyasaland,
Natal, Southern and Northern Rhodesia, how many
thousands of miles, how many towns, in more than two
years work for the John Wright Marionette Co. of London?

The tour ends somewhere near Salisbury. Exhausted,
tired of the company, we are going back to Johannesburg.

PART TWO

"'Are you ready, Friday?" said I. "Yes," says he. "Let fly, then," says I, "in the name of God!" and with that I fired again among the amazed wretches, and so did Friday; and as our pieces were now loaded with what I called swanshot, or small pistol bullets, we found only two to drop, but so many were wounded, that they ran about yelling and screaming like mad creatures, all bloody, and most of them miserably wounded...

"Now, Friday," says I, laying down the discharged pieces, and taking up the musket which was yet loaden, "follow me"; which he did with a great deal of courage; upon which I rushed out of the wood..."

Daniel Defoe: The Life and Adventures of Robinson Crusoe

I. 66 LOVEDAY STREET

Beginning again, jobless. We have managed to put by £200 from the tour. Jay in the Eastern Province with her parents.

Walking in Joubert Park, Johhanesburg, where the trams go by, clanging by up the hill into cosmopolitan Hillbrow. I am staying in the Shotley Hotel nearby, facing the park.

Tall Lombardy poplars agitated by the wind, tall blocks of flats in Hillbrow out of which come African nannies in white and blue uniforms and their charges, pampered Jewish children who have the run of this pleasure-ground. In the diningroom I share a table with three elderly woman. Miss Duller. Personal napkin rings and turkey every Friday. On Fridays I invest in a tin of Benson and Hedges.

An old wheezing female guest in the hotel foyer: 'I'm beginning to feel better, more like a human being, now that the summer's coming in.'

Nights are very cold and I have difficulty getting to sleep. Obliged to invest in an electric fire. Chill mornings. Temporary employment at Constantia Bookshop in Loveday Street. Mevrouw van Overbeeke (who owns the place) and Juffrouw Moon (in the order & dispatch department) are Dutch; Herr Hodge Melville and Herr Weltsch are German - the latter Jewish. Herr Weltsch formerly worked on the Berliner Tagblatt; he watched the Reichstag fire burning. A small, stooped man with pebble spectacles, a hypochondriac, married four times, allergic to snakes. He works over-time every evening, needlessly, spends the weekends in bed, all the windows of his flat bolted. His fourth wife, Rachel, groans at parties: 'Weltschian klein, time to go home. Time to come home, Weltschian klein!'

I am to take over Juffrouw Moon's job when she is on holiday. The foreign community of Johannesburg subscribe to Continental magazines: <u>Epoca,</u> <u>Quick,</u> <u>Tempo,</u> Marie <u>Claire,</u> <u>Domenica del Corriere.</u> Never err where <u>Kligger</u> and <u>Gluck</u> are concerned, Juffrouw Moon counsels me. (Are they miners, rich, irascible, set in their ways, who must not be crossed?) <u>Poetes d'Aujourd'hui;</u> <u>Morceaux choisis.</u>

Herr Weltsch on the telephone: 'Miss Moore? (interrogatory)...Miss Moore! (ingratiatingly). Ah Miss Moore (triumphantly)... I just laid my hand today on that book on Persian carpets.'

I just laid my hand. Trapping Methods for Bird Ringers. Constipation and Our Civilization (with Suggestions for Home Treatment). Pauper beginnings; Monday mornings in winter, stale air and customers farting.

II. 47 KAPTEIJNSTRAAT

I move again - to austere lodgings at 47 Kapteijnstraat, a small toy house presided over by a very fat and asthmatic Afrikaans woman, Mrs. Swannepoel. It's like a toy house with her in it; she fills it to overflowing. Obese and indolent, she spends most of her day in bed. The housework is done by a bony and elongated Zulu hexendoktor; his expression is severe, mask-like, and he has a bitter smell; he cleans and dusts the rooms and stairs, very louring - a forbidding manner. Mrs. S., looking out from behind the screen, rubicund, newspapers scattered all over her bed. All well upstairs? Yes, all well. And your wife? Yes, coming any day now.

Behind, on the walls, framed pictures of generations of cats and dogs.

Beginning again.

III. MY COLLEAGUES

Such strange colleagues. Hodge Melville is fair-haired, anaemic-looking, a placid, abstracted young gentleman; as a child when the war ended, he walked unlikely distances in Germany searching for his parents. Did he ever find them? He is in the accountancy section under Herr Weltsch.

A tsotsie pulled a gun on him in broad daylight, down

at the African bus terminus, and demanded money. Hodge
Melville, his thoughts miles away, brushed past him..

IV. SJAMBOK
Disquieting image: The maddened young policeman. The
African girl flying for her life. She races down the path
into darkness - the young constable, his belt loose, in hot
pursuit. A passing car goes grinding up the hill towards
the water-tower. From another, parked outside a block of
flats, a squat young man emerges, a sjambok in one hand,
his lip curling - retribution itself. No one sees; no one
stops or cares, it's late, darkness covers all.

V. STREET FIGHT
One evening, driving along Jeppe Street, we witnessed the
end of a knife-fight in one of the car-parks there - about as
public a place for it as, say, Cambridge Circus. Two
African women were fighting. One was bleeding heavily,
her dress hanging in flitters about her hips. They had one
weapon between them - a bread-knife. A circle of men
surrounded them, making no effort to interfere. The one
who was cut was screeching, naked from the hips up. A
long line of cars had stopped before the traffic lights.

They came to grips again, the injured one wailing at
the top of her voice; in the scuffle she wraps her legs
around the other and hauls away at her hair. They fall, the
knife dropping from the other's grasp. The injured one
takes it and jumps free. It seems likely now that murder
will be done. The men seem to think so too. As she runs
at the other, one of them takes her from behind; he pins
her arms to her side. She thrashes about, screeching, her
breasts wobbling and bloody.

Her opponent makes off, flying over by the pedestrian
crossing and away like the wind down one of the intersecting
streets leading to Bree Street.

The injured one frees herself and follows, bare-footed,
half-naked, bleeding profusely, running right through the
traffic which has begun to move again. She chases the other,
brandishing her breadknife, screeching. Her thin shoulder-
blades move in and out; she is brown and dusty with a

narrow compelling head, her ears pierced for small
brass earrings.

Brown and windowless, as though gutted by fire,
battered Non-European trams are rounding the corner by
Florian's Restaurant, entering cosmopolitan Hillbrow.

VI. ZOOLOGICAL NOTES

In the Johannesburg Zoo a dishevelled condor on its perch
shakes its soaked feathers, an ugly blue vein throbbing on
its bare skull. It thrusts its scrawny neck out, watches
through sluggish blood-filled eyes the jackdaws that come
and go out of its cage.

An outing of female white patients from a mental
institute sitting on the grass near the exit, staring about
them with freak stares. Their movements are stiff,
semi-paralysed.

The African men in smart city hats, sharp suits and
well-polished black shoes, laughing at the shameless
baboons; slapping themselves, mimicking the animals. A
pit of excrement, a laughing face.

Outside the Zoo, sprinting towards us in the bright sun,
a white man comes running with his topcoat thrown open,
a wideawake hat on the back of his head, glaring up at the
sky. High-stepping, he holds to his breast a framed picture
of the Sacred Heart. And so round the corner and out of
sight.

Autumn colours, dry sunshine of the high Rand.

VII. MUNTS

Cheating. The African garage attendant at Yeoville was
cheated of ten shillings by two of the Herrenvolk who drove
up for gasoline in a battered, mudcaked Dodge, up from the
Platteland. They swore they'd given the bleddy Kaffir man
a half note, man. But they didn't wait when he went for the
owner; drove off, cursing us and him.

VIII. BEGGARY AND DESTITUTION

An armless African beggar has a pitch by the lamp standard
at a corner near Jeppe Street post office. His charity box

is often empty. I have often wondered how he eats, since his arms are only stumps six inches long.

One day I saw an African boy bring him a double-decker sandwich from the Dutch delicatessen opposite the Monte Carlo Bio. The armless one watched me, rolling his eyes, the cornea brown and discoloured; the sandwich pressed up against his cheek, held in place by thrusting his shoulder up, and so brought it to his mouth in this manner. He gives me a haggard look for interrupting him at feeding time. Void heart, go on.

IX. STREET SCENES

(a) Africans at lunch-break, squatting on their haunches, their hands hanging, ape-like, loose at the wrists, over their knees, biding their time. They crouch there on spatulate feet, dusty and eroded in appearance, dressed in tatters: Java Man of 500,000 years ago. Crouching in Plein Street, in Market Street, Marshall Square, watching the action, the passers-by; sitting on the kerbside along Kruis Street playing cards or a rudimentary kind of draughts, using bottle caps, drinking tea from tin cans and stirring it with a wire clothes-hanger. A well-dressed one studying a text book on criminal law. When I question him he does not reply, looking up at me, but not deferential, rightly suspicious of Special Branch spies and informers.

(b) Another day outside the Supreme Court of Justice, during the second year of the interminable Treason Trial, an enigmatic figure stood near the side doors by the German cannons captured by South African troops in German South-West Africa. An elderly white eccentric dressed in a grey suit, with plus-fours, a workman's blue denim shirt, a black beret puffed up on his head, an eye-guard covering one eye; smoking a briar pipe and gazing about him in a frank open way, observing the Africans without apparent animosity. He had a rather flushed face, and one leg was up on the spoke-wheels of a cannon; surrounded by black tutelary spirits waiting there at the side door without much hope, in the rags and tatters of extreme poverty. One in a loose white shirt stands on crutches, his shoulders hunched up level with his ears so that he appears to be sprouting wings.

(c) Library Square: a hot griddle in summer. Haunt of
disreputable white drunks. They assemble here, brandy
drinkers and sherry drinkers, on seats reserved for
'Europeans Only'. Blankes, Nie-Blankes. In the winter they
hitch-hike to the Natal coast, these men and women with
discoloured faces, who act as contacts between the Africans
and the bottle-stores.

A Relation of Some Yeares' Travaile into Afrique, by
Sir Thomas Herbert (1634) in the City Library. The
troglodytes. In place of circumcision, the men pull away
'one ftone, fearing to beget too many children'. The women
give their children suck as they hang at their backs, 'the
vberous dugge ftretched ouer their fhoulder'. Mendelssohn
had a copy, formerly the property of Jonathan Swift.
Genesis of Gulliver?

In the hot griddle of the square, confronted by the
blackened faces of the drunkards, male and female, his
gloomy view of mankind does not seem too extreme.

X. A STABBING

The freelance commercial artist. His troubles that we are
now a party to. His wife divorced him and now has custody
of the two young children. He is convinced it's a frame-up
with the father-in-law (a lawyer) behind it; so stabs him in
the back and ends up under observation (the father-in-law
trying to have him certified, trying to get possession of his
car) in an institute. The lawyer, the ruthless one,
recovers. His victim moves to another flat; he works late
at night (it's a kind of neurosis with him). In one of the
flats below, facing his flat, another light burns late. The
commercial artist goes onto the balcony for a breath of
fresh air at four a.m. Another man is standing on the
balcony opposite, staring across. The father-in-law again!

The divorced wife re-marries (a Jew); the victimised
one takes the children every second Sunday. Sometimes this
doesn't work out. The father-in-law again. The son-in-law
by accident meets him, and is knocked senseless on the
path. His opponent is a champion middle-weight boxer.

Next the son-in-law is in prison for brandishing a

revolver before the ex-wife and the husband; the husband
runs from the room. The ex-husband very theatrically
threatens to kill himself. The ex-wife, protecting the
frightened children, phones for the police. He shows her
that the revolver is not loaded, then drops it in the
tank of his car. The police come; he meets them empty-
handed, all innocence. They find the revolver; he is thrown
into prison.

His background: The eldest in a Dublin Catholic family
of nine. The father at first indifferent to him, then becomes
attached to him. They quarrel 'because their characters are
so alike'. He emigrates to South Africa.

Seven years pass. He is travelling from Durban to
Johannesburg at night; travelling at about seventy he runs
over a horse asleep on the road. The front of the car is
smashed, and the horse in a bad way. He has a small pistol,
and fires three times into its head. The bullets bounce off:
he's hitting bone. He puts the gun at an angle to the
animal's ear and this time kills it.

He reached Johannesburg. That night he has a dream.
In the dream he sees his father, now grown old and frail,
going down the steep hill from Hillbrow. At the bottom,
where the gradient is even steeper, the old man is tottering,
almost running. The son follows him, crying out to him to
be careful. He sees his old father before him in a dressing-
gown tumbling over and striking his head a fatal wallop. The
son knows he's done for; he wakes up covered in sweat.

A couple of days pass, then a telegram arrives, sent
from Dublin and forwarded from Durban. It tells him what
he already knows: the father died on the same day and at
the same hour as the dream. (The son hasn't been home in
twenty years; he had the dream thirteen years ago).

XI. BIG MICK

His preposterous Ulster friend Big Mick is in engineering;
a muscular brute who suffers apparently from softening
of the brain: he repeats his yarns over and over again, in
the same room, to the same company. The wife, something
on the lines of Molly Bloom, florid, dressed to kill, her
overflowing bust strapped in with difficulty, her wobbly
rump, satin slippers - rather eccentric get-up. A stuffy

39

flat in which one suffocates. Parties of unimaginable
boredom. The grimaces of Big Mick waiting to be
'candidly' snapped lolling in his armchair, holding onto his
dentures. The armchairs all have chintz borders and seem
to be wading across the carpet. He once filed a story for
Time Magazine. He told us so himself, twenty times.

XII. MURDER IN HILLBROW

The impassive witness. Queers quarrelling; one shoots the
other three times in the chest and makes his escape down
the back stairs. A description of the dying man. - Shot
thrice, he crawls along the ground outside a first floor
flat, blood oozing through the back of his shirt, moving his
legs slowly sideways, his fingers in the cracks of the
ground; he seems to be 'fornicating with the cracks'.
Outside Ruth Levy's place. A witness hears the murderer
escaping down the stairs.

November 1958. Johannesburg. In this city, which
claims the highest suicide rate next to West Berlin, forty
a week died from unnatural causes. One double-locks at
night with a dead lock and lies awake listening to the
howling of the watch-dogs. City of watch-dogs.

XIII

Simmonds Street, Marshall Street, Hollard Street,
Syfret's Trust (Johannesburg Stock & Share Brokerage), the
Chamber of Mines, Marshall Square. The uncertainty of
beginning. Thin high cirrus masking the sun, but soon it's
blazing forth again; blue skies and warm air of the high
Rand, this marvellous winter climate. Nu-Nite Nitewear,
morning haze. Kahn's for pianos. Everything lightens and
tightens. The Republic is on its way. 'Killer Ape' showing
at the Bio-Cafe in Rissik Street. The tough ones lounging
outside. Stench of popcorn and Jeyes Fluid. Bawling of the
vocalist, electrified. Black Sash ladies outside the Town
Hall. A handful for the front. 'Wedding in Springtime' at
the Colosseum. Princess Margaret's wedding. 'Irma la
Douce' at the Brooke theatre. 111th performance.

One grows weary of the long sameness of the days
here. The only variety offered is the tropical storms which

recur punctually at five every evening; but even of these
one grows weary.

The roads, the commercial travellers, the quacks.
    Dr. Rex Ferris, specialist in Natuur-gemesing...
Asma...swak longe...breuk...stinkasem mangels...
katar....hardly wigheid...swak van du bloed...swak hart...
hare watuitval...abgesakte maag...slegtesukalasie...
Blindedermonetteking...

    XIV

An African burglar, small and sceptical, sitting on a bed,
holding up a mother and twenty-year-old daughter at gun-
point. Putting them through it. 'You tell me what white
woman in Jo'burg hasn't got a gun and jewels. Go on, you
tell me.' He locks them in the wardrobe, threatens to
shoot them through the door, and so makes his escape,
empty-handed. Then or later armed robbery carried the
death penalty, for Africans.

    XV. MARSHALL SQUARE

I have on a few occasions noticed an elderly white woman
of reduced circumstances standing at one of the corners of
the Square with an open suitcase in front of her on the
pavement. She is trying to peddle home-made dolls,
wretched objects priced at 5s. each. Nobody stops or looks
at them; I have never seen anyone buy from her. She
doesn't seem to mind. A patient bloodless face and unseeing
eyes, thinking of something else, wishing she were somewhere else. Remnants of former respectability apparent.
She wears the cast-off jacket of a man's blue suit, a
hobble skirt, dark blue, lower at the front than at the back;
on her head a bowl-shaped black raffia hat with a bull
hatpin thrust through the crown, a scarf wound about the
raffia. Tram-conductors pass her, those hard-faced
young men going off duty, caps on the backs of their heads
and their uniform jackets open. No one buys from her.

XVI. DREAM OF THE SNAKE AND THE AFRICAN

Looking through the kitchen into Isipingo Street. A group
of Africans surround something on the road. It's a snake.
One of them puts his boot down on its neck; the snake
coils itself about his leg, trying to spit its venom. Unable
to stamp directly on its head, he stumbles, and struggles
with the snake. They come nearer. I am terrified that the
snake will fall on Jay, then five or six months pregnant.

The snake, still coiled about the boot, now appears
outside the window (we are on the third or top floor in
Mount Willmar). It has a flat squashed head and looks
rather pathetic. On the point of falling not on Jay but on
me it murmurs, 'I'm done for... have pity!'

The snakes of terror hiss around your head, and
indeed around mine the snakes of fear hiss even wilder.

The day before, Todd Matshikiza and his coloured wife
came to lunch. His story of standing in a queue in front of
a scandalized Afrikaner at the snake-pit in Port Elizabeth.
Origin of the dream? A childless couple.

XVII. DAYDREAM

Heavy rain, a shattered window, a death here. The
murdered man with one arm inside. His body hangs outside, rain falls on his white shirt. Something that cannot
be altered. Grey ghosts; grey ghosts of human speech.

XVIII

23 March 1959. A day of bright sun in Johannesburg, with
autumn leaves everywhere. Die flowers away. Feeling
almost of Germany. The ring-tailed lemurs in their cage
in the Zoo alarmed by stirrings in the cage of vultures.
Complacent postures against the bars, their faces up to the
sun. Ra. They dangle their delicate hands. Eating paw-paw
rinds.

One night I drove with F. to Jan Smuts Airport to
meet her husband, who was flying from Cape Town. Harry
Oppenheimer was the first up the ramp off the Cape Town
flight. A few words in the baggage-man's ear and he departs
in his car; the rest of the passengers wait patiently for
their baggage to come up the escalator belt. The Cape

Town passengers standing about in the waiting hall on a
freezing night.

On the way back, we saw that an African had been run
over attempting to cross near a traffic robot. There was
some shattered glass on the roadway and a small crowd
about the injured man. Two in yellow crash helmets looking
at him and not saying a word. The injured man soaked in
blood; he lay half on the footpath and half on the road,
holding on for dear life, and made a weary gesture to us.

The jazz opera 'King Kong' at Witwatersrand University,
and Miriam Makeba doing bumps and grinds on the stage -
an African Maria Vivo. A 'mixed' audience; unprecedented
warmth of reception. This is a Jewish-African affair, and
the first movement towards a true national theatre in South
Africa. Stuttafords Non-European staff and the Non-
European staffs of Greatermans, O.K. Bazaars, Arnhold
& Co., Earthmoving Contractors, the Chamber of Mines,
Lipworth & Co., Joko Tea, and Adamczewski ('I am not
one of your Communist friends!') - all wish 'King Kong'
every success.

XIX

I go to work by the No. 11 bus into town, a 5d. ride, by
Gundelfinger & Weinraub, the Ord Tie Factory, Kahn's
Pianos, by the municipal tennis courts where a bored
coach in flannels and a peaked cap is lobbing brown balls
over the net to an uninspired novice. I see Sybil Joffe
getting out of her sister's dented car at 8.20 in the morning
of a fine sunny day outside J. Walter Thompson's agency.
I go on to 66 Loveday Street. Morning after morning.

On the morning bus. The bottom of Jeppe. Butcher's
boy (Bantu) cycling alongside the No. 11. A deep butcher's
basket with a severed bullock's head inside. Bristles about
the mouth, the eyes as if gouged out with a red-hot poker;
some fury of resignation about the flayed mouth: a skinned
death's head.

Looking down into the bedroom of one of the bungalows
adjacent to Mount Willmar one night, I saw a man kneeling
in his shirt and trousers by a double bed - sole support of

43

a white family of only modest means. His wife was sitting bolt upright by the wall, knitting, looking over at the husband every now and then. His eyes closed, he clasps his hands in sudden ardour, bowing his head humbly to the Almighty; Lord, Lord, have pity on such as I!

XX. SEANCE
Miss Kerk, rich, masculine-looking owner of cheese factory, a childless spinster, adopts three children - Elizabeth, Noel and Jemma.

They grow up. Noel, 'a bit retarded', found employment as an overseer on the roads. Elizabeth married; the husband was a good-for-nothing who used to beat her. She had two children by him. The husband beat her when she was pregnant with her third. In the nursing home in her delirium she was crying out, 'Oh don't hit me! Please don't hit me on the back!' She died in childbed and the baby with her.

When she was dying she extracted a promise from Miss Kerk that she would look after the two children. The husband was not allowed to have custody of them, so the Child Welfare Association ruled.

Then the spirit medium Alec Harris came to Johannesburg, and Miss Kerk went to see him. At the seance he successfully invoked the spirit of the dead wife. She materialised and went straight to Miss Kerk, took both her hands and laid her cheek against Miss Kerk's, calling her 'Markie' - her old pet name for her - thanking her for all she had done and was still doing for her two children, and this with great feeling.

The scene of pine, eucalyptus and peppergum at Observatory, an accumulation of scents; the warm wind, dry eucalyptus - a memory of Cavtat in Dalmatia. We have a child now - a little boy; he cries out under the trees, looking up from his pram.

On the hillside above the golf course the African Zionist sects are singing and parading. It's a very energetic religion; they march and counter-march among the trees near the Benoni Road - the choral chanting of the bearded priests, their deep voices raised in prayer, promises, objurgation. The female supplicants answer with their thin banshee wail. A canticle of psalms, a brotherhood of the

44

bushes, the voice of Africa at its lamentations. A
multitude of insects rise over the grass; it's evening time,
the sun going down over the hill. The insects show up
palely, agitated; the golfers are going home. The singing
and the insects rise together, the golfers neither seeing the
one nor hearing the other. We dream of living elsewhere...
on St. Helena, in the Seychelles. Endless life; endless
choice.

The pedigree dogs in the ornate suburban haciendas
along Urania Street bark at us, the same as at all
intruders. The sun-drenched Daughters of Jerusalem are
showing off their brown legs. The sprinklers revolve and
revolve on the green lawns, widening their skirts of spray.
Peaceful days in Johannesburg.

XXI. MORGAN AND McGAW

I am employed by a company that produces and markets
short commercial advertising films. I am in the Scenario
Department with my colleague de Wet.

We work in a shabby room on the sixth floor of a block
of office buildings near the junction of Market and Kruis.
My salary is adequate. In the office is a battered green
filing cabinet, three desks (one connected to the General
Manager's office by an intercom.), an unshaded electric
light that on winter days shines on bare and not particularly
clean lemon-yellow walls. I am to spend a year here and
save £800.

My immediate predecessor, I am told, was a
drunkard. I never met him. I share the office with this
weepy lunatic de Wet. Despite his Afrikaans name he
affects a very pure BBC accent. He is on the phone
throughout the day on matters of an excruciatingly private
nature, weeping into the receiver, pleading for his
happiness and whatever remains of his sanity to be returned
to him - inanities of that nature. He is divorced, but has
got himself engaged to another girl, though uncertain whether
he should go through with it. He seems to enjoy sending her
flowers. However, it comes to nothing. This thin, pale,
sickly-looking fellow is both very conceited, where women
are concerned; and deeply neurotic, where his chances with
them are concerned. He will leave a few months after my

arrival.

His successor, McGaw, is hardly an improvement.
McGaw has the identical BBC-announcer accent as de
Wet, the identical fastidious intonation. Edinburgh-born,
with a failed career in advertising behind him. He is
portly and middle-aged, with stooped shoulders, a bad
complexion and red-rimmed eyes. He has run to fat, has
a great beaked nose, and is very nervous. A balding pate
and an indecisive manner; wears spectacles, is gallant
with the ladies; has an awkward flaccid deportment,
rolling and pitching on uncertain feet, shoulders bowed and
eyes to the ground. Not in his health. A reformed
alcoholic. Market Street knows him.

He makes his job seem very difficult. He uses a
topheavy office Underwood, single spacing on yellow copy
paper, correcting his scripts in pencil (second thoughts)
and ball-point (third and fourth thoughts). He is not very
good at his job and - what's more to the point - is far
from adroit in his handling of the General Manager.

XXII. McGAW'S TICS
A hacking cough, developing into convulsions, chewing
boiled sweets, visiting the w.c. twenty five times a day,
opening the window to read the time off Mosenthal's clock
fifteen times a day, grinding his molars (another boiled
sweet), restlessly shifting his position on the leather
seat of his swivel chair, yawning, wiping his spectacles.

He lives in fear and dread of the buzzer going: a
summons from the tyrannical General Manager to have his
script subjected to severe scrutiny. Morgan the GM bullies
and harries him whenever he can.

The buzzer goes; McGaw draws in his breath, swallows,
pushes down the button, says 'Yes, Mr. Morgan.' Tyrant
Morgan's acid voice says: 'McGaw - come in, will you?'

The squeaking of his swivel chair. It has a pin loose.
Every fourth or fifth day, for light relief, it comes loose;
McGaw then upends it and struggles with it on the floor.
Then he has to go and wash his hands. De Wet was hardly
ever in the office; McGaw is hardly ever out of the w.c.

He perspires a lot, wipes his forehead constantly with
Kleenex, yawns his head off, removing his heavy-rim

spectacles to pluck at his albino eyelashes, yawns his
prodigious watery yawn, and then stoops again over his
scored and much-amended yellow script, already two days
overdue. Would it do?... would it ever do?

His nerves are on edge, and he cries out involuntarily
when objects fall: the sudden smash of a saucer on the floor
makes him start from his chair and cry out. Morgan
continues to humiliate and harry him.

Mr. Morgan is in the moviola room viewing a rough-
cut and wishes to see Mr. McGaw! - the message comes
through the private secretary. McGaw, with the memory of
recent humiliations fresh in his mind, tacks from side to
side down the detested corridor, his shoulders hunched,
leering at the switchboard girl as he passes her open door;
he holds in one hand sheets of yellow copy paper, added to
and held together with clips, the whole typed in cramped
single spacing and corrected with pen and pencil in his
meticulous handwriting. Mr. Morgan is in a wax in the
moviola room.

XXIII. OSLO
Mrs. Gramm is a small, tubby lady, a Lithuanian Jewess,
who works in another department, is sometimes available
as a relief copy typist. Morgan is very particular about the
appearance of scenarios and requires eight carbons. Mr.
Morgan, who knows everybody's business better than they
do themselves, goes over the firm's books with Mrs.
Gramm. She does not care much for him. Her own husband
was a quiet, dependable, studious man; they lived in Oslo.
'Quisling was my husband's riding-master,' she says with
pride.

XXIV. THE SWITCHBOARD GIRL
The swaggering bum of the young switchboard girl. She
has a good figure, wears very tight clothes. Her boyfriend
is in the police. He's a patrol cop. Sometimes he calls.
- A hard-faced young Afrikaner in black leather leggings
and castoff S.S. uniform, blonde hair cropped to the roots.
He'll take no nonsense.

This girl is also bullied by tyrant Morgan. She weeps

47

at the switchboard, her eyes swim behind thick
lenses: 'Mr. Morgan is no gentleman.'

XXV. McGAW AGAIN

Cold mornings on the sixth floor. The dry fug from the
electric fire. In the resounding canyon of Kruis Street
below us furniture is being dragged across the pavement
and into new business premises, with a harsh grating noise
like the roaring of lions. McGaw buffets open the window to
stare at Mosenthal's clock and cold air comes in.

The GM is away on business, driving hard bargains in
Cape Town. 'I think I'm hep,' McGaw says, 'but I suppose
the young people of today would consider me hopelessly
square.' Another prodigious watery yawn engulfs him and
his weak, red-rimmed eyes fill with tears; he wipes his
eyes and nose with the corner of a Kleenex, pulling down
his albino eyelashes. A boredom scarcely to be tolerated,
witnessed or endured. McGaw's spongy feet, hacking
cough, damp, damp hands.

O. Rubenstein, J.B. Pain, the Mental Health Society
of the Witwatersrand, African Underwear Manufacturers -
these names in turn are revealed to me. The lift stops -
it's the ground floor; I get out with the others.

The streets, the evening light and heat, the bus-ride
back to the flat. Liberation. Evenings on the balcony with
Kensington mine-dumps in the distance. Drinking gin.

Going to work in the morning, walking along Kruis
Street, I see a familiar figure in front, shambling along
on his bear's feet, it's like locomotor ataxy - McGaw en
route to further humiliations.

XXVI. EROS

Sharply defined morning shadows in the intervening gardens
separating our block of flats from another block across the
way. Morning after morning the sun shines on a second
floor bedroom. Morning after morning a figure appears at
the window to exercise naked after showering. Dark haired
and pale skinned. The husband, a shadowy figure, moves
in the background.

XXVII

Mornings in the Scenario Department when business is
slack, or the free and easy times when the General
Manager is away on business, driving hard bargains in
Capetown, Durban, Port Elizabeth. McGaw relaxed.

'Chaps, do you realize that this time ten years ago I
was burning archives in the gardens of the British Embassy
at Liege? (peering at his desk calendar)...the 10th of May.'

My colleague who sucks - or rather <u>grinds</u> - boiled
sweets throughout the day, for his nerves; visits the Gents
fifteen to twenty times a day, for his incontinent bladder;
who lives in dread of the General Manager.

'As I grow older I give less and less credence to the
doctrine of Christian Science, though I believe their
findings in psychoanalysis are sound enough.' Wisdom of
McGaw.

I said: Yes, but didn't Roman Catholicism make this
discovery several centuries ago? 'Where, pray?' (raising
a sceptical eyebrow). In the confessional, I say.

XXVIII. SUNDOWNER BAR

The Sundowner Bar is in Jeppe Street next door to
Pilgrim's Bookshop. It has an undistinguished facade, with
two entrances. I go to the Saloon Bar during the ninety
minute lunch break for purposes of meditation, and for the
very good Hansa draught lager. It's chilled, and comes from
Windhoek - a real German lager. It's a quiet bar, rather
cramped, and might well serve as a stage model for the
bar in <u>The Iceman Cometh.</u> The counter rather cramped
too; the roof low, supported by imitation wooden pillars,
with a fine cheating grain; a narrow place with real
'operatic' German barmen, stout and flushed, Hans and
Richard - Chianti bottles on the wall and a fresco of Ludwig
II's Schloss Linderhof. My eyes have gone up and down
that lake, have hunted in that forest, oh hundreds of times.

The place is frequented by sallow-faced window-
dressers, White drunks, riff-raff that this city glories in.
Every day for more than a year I went there; it made
Johannesburg tolerable for me. They served hot soup free
on cold days.

The three regulars. Dr. X, a Jew, qualified doctor,

late of London, a hole-in-the-heart expert, very hard on the bottle. Some illegal practice perhaps? Abortion? He dresses in a dark morning suit with a waistcoat into the pockets of which he likes to put his fingers; a derby hat pushed onto the back of his head; very waspish.

The second member of the trio is an Austrian Count, very distinguished-looking, tall, well dressed; his habit of asking questions (sign of intelligence?). Before the war he worked for Skoda, the Czech munitions firm. He was in China when the war broke out, and came back via Mozambique; passing through the Union he was interned, and spent six years in a camp outside Johannesburg. Hans, the stout barman from Westphalia, tells me all this. He was interned with the Count, and recalls the other's internee's pyjamas with coronets stitched on the breast. He is less far gone in drink than the other two; wears an Anthony Eden hat, very tall, brown-faced man, a moustache, speaks English with a German accent, a cutting edge. The type one sees on the polo field. Always full of schemes for getting wealth (gold?) out of the ground; schemes invariably crushed by the doctor.

The third member of the party is small, monkey-faced Irishman out of Cahirciveen, his features dark and his hands shaking from constant heavy brandy-drinking. Fitzy. He left Ireland twenty years ago to seek his fortune in Johannesburg. His hopeless, bleary eyes; telling me a story concerning Wilde, of doubtful authenticity. Suspected homo leanings, more out of hopelessness than nature. Manages - fiddles? - the books for the taxi drivers on the rank outside the bar. They are inseparable; sometimes arriving by taxi, already a quarter shot; they never touch solids for lunch, but put down six or seven double brandies. Their range of interests is exceptional; inquiries put out by the Count, countered by the Jewish wiseacre, Fitzy plodding after, a long way from Cahirciveen. Fugitives from Nightwood.

The relief barman George is a shady character, not all in it; member of the Deaf, Dumb & Blind Association of South Africa, he has travelled the country from end to end, as have I. Some curious beliefs. He hears voices. A furtive, weasel-like, undependable man.

G (furtively, behind his hand): I got the message again.

I: Yes?

G: 'Jet Stream'. It's a certainty. Put your money on now. Nine to one. 'Jet Stream'.

(He talks in spurts like this, like Mr. Jingle.)

I: I never back horses.

G (reassuringly): That's all right. Try 'Jet Stream'.

I (wary): Who gave you the message?

George serves a customer a bottle of milk stout. Comes up to me again, leaning forward, fixing me with his no-coloured eyes.

G (with much conviction): I got it from another world, Sir.

I: Which world?

G (radiant): The one we all go to after this one, Sir.

Long pause. George goes away; comes back.

I: But are the spirits of the other world interested in what goes on in this one? Are they interested in horses?

G (very solemn, in measured tones): Sir, I assure you (leaning forward, giving me a blast up from his sour stomach), the spirits never lied to me. And they gave me great help all my life. Gawie (the Afrikaans owner of the Sundowner) put on £5 this morning and I put on £8. A certainty! 'Jet Stream.'

Stout Hans from Westphalia glaring at him in flushed amazement.

XXIX

After a stormy scene McGaw is ignominiously sacked by tyrant Morgan - for general incompetence, slackness of application, incompatability of temperament with the boss.

Some few weeks later I encounter him again, dressed in a white coat standing at a street corner, attempting to sell Bibles; he expresses himself well satisfied with the open-air employment. Sinking, sinkingly.

XXX. JOB RESERVATION LAW

The African lift boys have been fined and their places taken by a set of incompetent Afrikaner harridans with stiff, henna'd hair-do's, conscripted from the lower stratas of S.A. society. They sit on the job, on small

stools provided, talk as equals to their passengers, drink
endless bottles of Coca-Cola, and have difficulty stopping
the lift flush with whatever floor you want to get out on.
They are of the same breed as the girls in mauve uniforms
who work in the Film Room - as motley a crowd as you
might hope to come across in all this remarkable Sub-
Continent.

The Africans, decent, sober young men, have no
alternative but to go; they leave without complaining, and
without any alternative employment offered them.

J.B. Pain, the Mental Health Society of the Witwatersrand -
a couple in the lift, mother and grown son, exchange a
very wild look; the son's fixed stare, inimical glance of
paranoia, the mother's hair standing on end, as if in a high
wind; they go hand in hand down the corridor leading to
the Mental Health Society of the Witwatersrand.

XXXI. COALBROOK
In January 1960 at Coalbrook Mine, 435 miners (6 White)
were entombed in a fall-in at 500 feet and buried alive,
none were ever recovered.

In June there occurred the death of George Siwisa,
leader of the banned Pan-African Congress, serving a
three-year sentence for incitement, in Boksburg Gaol. On
the death certificate the cause of his death was made out as
'brain thrombosis'. He was buried next day by Cinderella
Prison officials.

Three weeks later his daughter received a letter from
the Bantu Commissioner's office in Pretoria addressed to
'the relatives of the late George Siwisa, ' and requesting
that his clothes be removed.

Coming back hazily through the cut flowers of the
Indian flower market behind the Supreme Court of Justice,
I see a police van driving away from the door with the arms
of African prisoners thrust through the bars at the back
giving the freedom Africa sign, and muffled cheering from
inside the van.

XXXII. A WEEKEND AT FERNDALE
It was two o'clock in the morning and we were alone in the

Mauthners' place at Ferndale. I woke up knowing it was going to happen. A moment later I heard the smash of the long window in the lounge being broken.

The bungalow, a German architect's home, had been broken into two years previously and ransacked. They didn't want that to happen again while they were away, and so had asked us would we like to stay there for the long weekend. Ferndale is some distance outside the city on the Green Line bus route; a sparsely populated area where well-to-do professional people have built houses. I had been sitting all day reading Gibbon in the garden and drinking cold Lion beer. After darkness fell the mosquitoes came in great numbers (the fishmoths were already there in the house - something to do with the water supply). The rooms were very small and stuffy with not a breath of air circulating. We couldn't open the windows once the burglar alarm was set; neither could we sleep under the mosquito netting.

After the window was smashed, we weren't sure that the alarm would work. Jay pressed all the buttons. The alarm started; it went on and on, wailing. Then silence. Not a sound. I thought, 'They're all inside, waiting with their guns out.' I wanted ten minutes then unlocked the bedroom door, went along the hall, opened the livingroom door, switched on the light. There was nobody there. I pulled back the drapes. The long window was broken down its length. Someone had tried to get in; there was the brick.

That bright sunny day, sitting in the garden drinking Lion beer, looking at the rolling countryside, the blue mountains where we'd gone climbing - the Magaliesburg - with the vines turned yellow, syringa leaves, I thought they would come back to finish what they'd started.

When it was dark again we sat there reading with the drapes pulled back and the window broken so that a troop of them could walk in, if they wanted to. We didn't set the alarm, and spent a very uncomfortable night, waiting for the blow on the back of the head, like the pigmy man in the fairy tale. Next day the Mauthners came back.

XXXIII. SHABEEN
There's one in Bellevue near the water tower on a ridge overlooking Bez Valley on one side and the area around

McKay Park and its Lombardy poplars, uniformed African
nannies and pampered over-fed Jewish children. It's close
to a municipal refuse dump that had been out of use for
some time, and overgrown with bluegum and peppergum
trees, with the rusted bodies of three or four cars that
had been left there to rot. On non-working days the
Africans went there, dressed in their best clothes, to drink
Kaffir beer - Basutu and Zulu, Amaxosas and Bantus in
slick city suits, white shirts, highly polished black shoes;
their women dressed in very full gathered, slate-grey
skirts, their hair cut very short and wearing knitted woollen
caps brought into fashion by Miriam Makeba. All compor-
ting themselves with much dignity, hardly ever drunk, the
women staying in the background, ladling the thick beer
into billy-cans. The men squat on their heels or on the
rusted cars, holding smoke-blacked tin cans in their pale-
palmed hands; sitting about there on the rocks, on the look-
out for the police (illegal for Africans to drink in White
areas, illegal to have shabeens), or in the shade of the
bluegum trees, calling out to their friends who pass by on
the road.

XXXIV. GAMBLING

There's a gambling school recess in Wyncliff Road. It's a
short cul-de-sac made up of blocks of expensive flats on
the left, terminating at the white palings before a mock
colonial Spanish edifice with front patio, geraniums,
carriage lamps on the white wall. We often call on friends in
Samedo there and have noticed this old battered Hudson
always standing outside and the flat-boys sitting around it
and in it. They are always hanging about there in their
hours off duty; the car never seems to be driven anywhere.

It's one of the spoils of a big poker game.

The flat-boys are inveterate gamblers and play for
high stakes. They put down a year's pay on a single game.
The Hudson is always changing hands, but whoever wins it
is afraid to drive it away. The gamblers who have owned
it and lost it, sit on it or near it, touching it, waiting for
their luck to change. So it remains where it is, weighed
down by the weight of the gamblers. They wear the
conventional 'flat-boy's' uniform, the white cotton vest

and knee-length pants with blue edgings that is the uniform
of their bondage: a kind of light opera convict garb. And
bare-footed.

Their life, however, is no light opera; at night we
hear the raids, the boots on the fire escape, the police
whistles, the crying and the bare feet running. We wait
for gun shots. These raids are carried out in the early
hours of the morning and are engineered by the ever-
vigilant Special Branch, anxious to apprehend treasonable
persons, Commies, black whores, run-of-the-mill infrin-
gers of the notorious Pass Laws.

Sitting on a dentist's chair on the sixteenth floor of
an office building in the centre of Johannesburg, a view of
flat roof-tops and washing blowing on lines, a flag pole
with the Union Jack flying in the breeze, and on a distant
mine dump away towards Benoni, a white scarf of mine
dust blowing off the rim.

As and from tomorrow the British flag will be brought
down and the new flag of the free Republic run up in its
place. 'Out of the blue sky...' Die Stem. While I'm in the
chair his ex-wife the novelist Nadine Gordimer phones to
ask the dentist the meaning of being 'on the threshold of
pain'. Gavronski tells her all about the threshold of
pain.

XXXV. THE AIR OF THE RAND
This quite wonderful and invigorating air, and the blue,
blue skies of the high Rand. Portuguese East market
gardeners. Thin high cirrus masking the sun briefly. A
wild swan flying over the skyscrapers of Johannesburg; it
must have mistaken it for a forest; no, it's a city - it
turns back.

Martin de Kock in the Sundowner Bar. Folk wisdom.
Baboons when shot cry like human babies. A remedy used
against their pilfering used by the farmers is to catch one,
paint him white and let him loose again. Gregarious by
nature, he runs for the herd. Terrified by his startling
colour they flee from him; he can never catch up with them
and dies of loneliness.

Karin the young Lesbian has eyes of an ocelot.

Looking down from the 20th floor at City Heights at the sun-tanned beauty in the red bikini sun-bathing beside the kidney shaped swimming pool full of blue water, reflecting clouds passing high above City Heights, the sun blazing in mid-heaven.

Dapper brown-faced Portuguese East businessmen alighting from a train in the main rail terminal. One, very distinguished looking, in a dark suit, spotless white shirt, carries a cane on the crown of which is pinned an orchid. If certain words were said to an old stick it would be covered in flowers and leaves and would take root again. Kandogya-Upanishad.

A train made up of many carriages, being pushed from behind by two engines, steam-driven, panting and struggling with difficulty through an ascending chain of mountains.

The White lunatics on the Zoo grass; their stiffened bodies and faces. Lunacy. Paranoiacs. A kind of paralysis of the inner self. Nothing sadder than this reality. The giant condor, stiff with age, with resentment, has an ugly blue vein that throbs on his skull; he will not offer to spread out his bedraggled and tawdry wings. Captivity weighs him down. Years of confinement have deadened his spirits. His eyes are filled with blood.

'Nous fumons tous ici l'opium de la grande altitude, voix basse, petit pas, petit souffle.'

All of us smoke the opium of high altitude here, with low voices, short steps, short breaths.

And in this year alone, 1960, 16 territories in Africa, with 85 million inhabitants, became independent.

The brunette's exercises in the nude still go on; a resplendent bare white figure exposed to the morning sun - a white goddess behind glass. Juno's love back and mesial groove.

One fine morning, looking down through the leaves and electric blue Canterbury bell-shaped jacaranda blossoms, from the upper deck of a No. 11 bus, I recognized her below, standing in the queue, fully dressed. Very proper, wearing a belt, haughty, attractive-looking, pitch-black hair, rather stern, partly unrecognisable. Unknowable shape, living statue.

Sardines swim always towards the sun; so to catch

them you must get to the east of them in the morning,
and to the west of them in the afternoon.

XXXVI
A well-built young beauty in a white pleated skirt that
clings to her hips and outlines her rangy thighs, a
suggestion of briefs underneath, and the classic amphora-
outline of the female lower torso, intimations of
considerable sexual prowess, a tight fit, walking alone in
Joubert Park of a summer evening.
    Field research.
    The handsome couple sitting on a bench under the trees
in the little steeply inclined park at the top of Stuart Drive.
The woman has a bouffant hair-style, her thick black hair
piled up on top of her head; she wears a dark red corded
jacket and a close-fitting purple-brown tweed skirt, showing
a lot of leg. She might be Yugoslav. The man is dressed in
a dark suit with a white shirt; he might be Italian or French.
They are a striking couple. A little boy of about three is
with them. He stands a little way off and watches them. They
are embracing. The child watches them embracing. He is
told to go away and play. He goes away but soon is back
again, staring at them. The woman takes him on her knees.
The huddle of the three of them together. Bare trees,
late evening sun, the last light dying on the mine dumps
beyond Bez Valley. Hot love 6,000 feet up. The supplicants;
sure I must perish by your charms unless you take me in
your arms.

Hot days; leaves falling about the Donald McKay Park,
the poplars turning silver-white in the rising wind. Afternoon showers of torrential rain. Dry here all summer, now
the rains come in the autumn; and every day the pictures
slip a little more off square on the walls, following another
fall-in down in the mines.

XXXVII. BAGLEY
A new man in the Scenario Department. New blood. Bagley.
A small faded person in sagging trousers. He seems to be
covered in a kind of grey lichen. Short strutting walk,

precise manner, partly bald, with a rash of eczema on his
temples, impossible to say whether his hair is his own or
not; wears the one dark morning suit, bi-focals, sports a
goatee beard. A look of Trotsky. Very muddy complexion,
and a fearful impediment in his speech. Why does Morgan
hire these freaks? There are three of us in the department
now, all with the same starved anxious look, and all with
goatee beards. My other colleague, Egaltine, puts out
occasional verse and helps to edit a magazine devoted to
the arts, for the Meat Board.

Bagley himself deserves some space. He is an ex-
journalist on the Rand Daily Mail. He worked for
Laurence Gander. Very sanguine manner with Morgan.
Exactly the wrong way to treat him. The boss, masking
his venomous nature, is all politeness to him. I cannot
see this state of affairs lasting. His hilarious attempts to
pronounce 'Chamonix' over the telephone.

The goatee-bearded Scenario Department walking at the
double after the dapper General Manager, rounding the
corner of Kruis Street and disappearing into a cinema,
entering a small private theatre in the bowels of the
cinema, to study and comment on pre-release screenings
of the department's day-to-day output. International
prize-winning advertising films. I Sha-sha-sha...I show-
show-show...shash-shassh-shasssshsshzz... Chamonixer!
Go to. Tongue-tied. Tu-quoque.

Bagley's tics: one leg crossed over the other in a
fussy way, agitated in the air, humming. Picking his
thoughtful upper lip with a thoughtful thumb and forefinger
and letting it smack back into place (signifying what?).
Clicking in and out (sometimes at twenty minutes at a
stretch) the retractable point of his BIC pen. Very cross-
looking when contradicted - a myopic glare directed at me.
Small somewhat conceited man. Omniverous reader. A
book always on his desk. Atlas Shrugged, by Ayn Rand.

XXXVIII. MR. ALLEN

An old drunken White falling off a No. 11 bus at a stop in
Isipingo Street. Some of the passengers reach out as if to
help him. Those who are getting off have almost to jump

over him. He lies there, holding his heart. Jay and a
young man help him to his feet. He has hurt his head.
'Oh I have lived too long', an old drunk of seventy-six who
lies on his back on the pavement, staring up at them. 'Let
me lie.'

They take him to Netherely House, a home for indigent
old men. It's some way back from the road with a fore-
court of candystripe pillars, red and white, ferns, a turkey
cock scratching its wings on the cement floor, and in the
background more old men hobbling about in the gloom. It's
like looking into an aquarium.

Poor Bagley near tears. As suspected, tyrant Morgan has
set about breaking his spirit, and with predictable results.
Humiliating script conference.

Dream: The racing savage, the thick foliage, puff of
gunsmoke from the tunnel in the forest. The carcass of a
wild beast - boar or bear? wild hog? - being hauled out
by the hind legs. Signifying what? Years dreams return;
I am another now, and yet the same.

XXXIX. A JOURNAL OF THE TERROR

Reading a book with that title in the City Library. An
account of the occurrences in the Temple during the
confinement of Louis XVI, by Monsieur Clery, the King's
valet-de-chambre, together with a description of the last
hours of the King by the Abbe de Firmont. Folio Society,
1955.

'We were scarcely seated when a head on the point of a
pike was held to the window...the head was of the Princess
de Lamballe's, which, though bleeding, was not disfigured,
and her fine light hair, still curling, waved round the pike.

The body of the Princess de Lamballe, naked and bloody
as it had been dragged from the prison de la Force to the
Temple...

The person that carried it was mounted upon the
rubbish of some houses that were ordered to be pulled
down for the purpose of isolating the Tower: another stood
behind, holding the heart of the unfortunate Princess,
covered with blood, on the point of a sabre.'

In the massacre of September, 1792, over 1,000 men

and women were done away with, some of them with great
cruelty.

Bagley's departure.

XL. SHARPEVILLE
March 21st, 1960. Anti-Pass Law demonstration in
Vereeniging. The police, with Saracens in support, fired
on and killed 69 African demonstrators, men and women,
wounding 186.

March 24th. Smell of sickness in the deserted Sundowner
Bar. Later the regulars drift in. The subdued brandy-drinker
orders another Commando from Richard, as he has been
doing for months, years, on end. Beginning to show in his
face. Immersed in his Rand Daily Mail as usual.

Of the 186 wounded, 38 are at Vereeniging Hospital
and 148 at Baragwanath Hospital; over 70 per cent of the
wounds were in the back and so terrible that it was thought
dum-dum bullets were used by the police. These wounds
were in fact caused by 'tumbling' bullets coming from Sten
guns fired continuously without pauses between bursts.

On one of the ominous days after Sharpeville, a time of
dire portents when the long-threatened seemed about to
come at last, a rumour was circulating to the effect that a
mob of Africans were marching from the locations on
Johannesburg. The old woman, Anna, our washerwoman
from Orlando, I knew was in the flat with Jay; I decided
not to phone, and went back to work.

Morgan, who prided himself on his fair treatment of
his own African servants, had an automatic pistol out on
his desk and some rounds of ammunition. 'If I have to go, '
he said, mock-histrionic, 'I'll take some of them with me. '
His secretary scuttled from the room 'Oh, Mr. Mor-GAN!'

The rest of that peculiar day. The feeling that we were
on the edge of civil war, that one might perhaps not live
beyond tomorrow, that Jay and the child would die, was
like a hand of ice.

After work the city cleared fast, a rapid exodus to the
suburbs, leaving the centre of the city deserted. African
newspaper boys were flying through the streets on their
bicycles and flinging down the late editions at the feet of

the remaining White bus queues, like insolent pages come
from the enemy lines with bold ultimatums.

But the Star reported nothing of an undisciplined horde
marching on Johannesburg, no picture of the bloodied head
of the Princess de Lamballe on the end of a pike; it
reported only common everyday occurrences. The beautiful
Miss Antoinette Botha photographed at the pottery exhibition
of Henk Jacobs and Harry Duys.

On the way home, the bored tennis coach, still in
flannels and peaked cap, still lobbing brown tennis balls
over a net at the municipal hard courts to a very
unaccomplished male novice at the game.

XLI. GLISSADE

April 21st. A month after Sharpeville, and the blood-
stains still on the road. I ask Lewis Nkose, 'What kind of
man is Colonel Spengler?' 'Spengler?' he says. 'He is a
butcher. He has the face of a butcher.'

He speaks of the sweetish smell of blood that you could
smell, after the shooting. He was there.

The air is full of flying mine dust. I have an inflamed throat
and retire to bed at about nine, feeling wretched. Mourning
air of forgotten childhood mingled with premonitions of
one's last end. Evening benediction begins; night falls, out of
the craters rises the mists. Knowing nothing, believing
nothing; live a little longer, if you can. I have this disturbing
dream: I am flying in the Alps with six others. We are
dressed as for skiing. Our arms extended, like gliders we
fly about in the thin rarefied air, our shadows following us
below on the virgin snow. It's high up in the Alps. I am
there, drifting about. Someone calls, 'Feel the snow! It's
like fire.' I sail down and kick up some with my bare feet.
Yes, like fire.

There is a high escarpment that no one can clear. I
attempt it, but it's impossible, the face is too steep.

In the Alpine hut one of the party has cut himself by
accident. There's not much blood, but nevertheless he
says he must return to the base. He leaves immediately. A
pair of scissors lie on the table. I take them up and cut
myself deeply on both wrists. Great clots of blood stain

the walls and the snow near the door. I've severed an
artery; the blood goes on pumping out. I am weakening; it's
I who have done this, yet I seem to be standing outside
myself. I watched 'myself' do it: 'him' I take for myself.

A Johannesburg Star photograph of the 'weapons' used by
the African insurgents at Sharpeville. In 40-45 seconds of
firing, so many killed, so many wounded, so much blood.
A pile of knobkerries, sticks, stones. Like what?
    Windfalls in a winter wood.

PART THREE

21st July, 1960. Last day in Johannesburg. Main railway terminal. Train for Blaney and East London. We sail from there on the 28th. I read of ten Africans killed and four injured, three seriously, in a faction fight between Mbonos and Ngulubenis at Maritzburg.

The taciturn soldier. Kliptown, Midway, Lenz, the locations out of Johannesburg. A week's holiday in King William's Town ahead. Jay has gone ahead there to her parents three weeks previously.

Kidd's Beach, Eastern Province. We rent a house near the beach. The breathing of the cattle at night. Generally deserted beaches. The coloured youths dancing like dervishes naked on the dunes; their swaying stallions' erections. The two African girls coming in their city finery. They all go swimming together. Scrummages in the surf. Their cries.

The lagoon. Deep coughing of the baboons among the laurels. Days alone there. The dog swimming in the estuary early in the morning. The Bantu girls coming with their fancy men. Putty-coloured skin of the Cape Malays, with deformed features, like lepers. In the evenings we buy brandy, for 15s. a bottle.

Jay's dream: 'It's a big hotel next to the railway lines. My mother and I have a big room on the second floor. I'm trying to pack but she keeps on emptying the suitcase. She is discontented and moves from room to room spreading the clothes about.

On our side of the building and directly in front of the hotel four oil tanks stand, delicate quadrupeds with their four big balls on the top standing about a hundred feet off the ground.

There's a revolution in the city. The first oil tank is set on fire above our heads. It explodes in flames. There is a terrific outcry in the hotel, with guests screaming out

of windows and running through the rooms. I run to my
mother, but she is so petulant she doesn't care. I look
everywhere for the suitcase. She's hidden it. I ask her
where it is; she says she doesn't know. I hear people
running past the hotel and shouts outside. Then I find
the suitcase. I begin to pack in a hurry. My mother keeps
taking the clothes out and throwing them on the bed.

The second oil tank is now on fire. I hear the
roaring of the flames and black particles of steel and ash
are falling past the windows. Try as I can, the suitcase
always remains empty. Outside, we see the flames going
straight up. There was a man there. I knew he was there.
I shout to a friend to go and help him. There are two of
them after him, and I can see him clearly lying on his
stomach under the third oil tank, which he is about to set on
fire.

As he reaches up he is shot from behind through the
back of the head. Dying, he goes on making the gesture of
pulling a lever, unmindful that it's someone else who moves
his hand.'

28th July, 1960, East London docks. The Warwick Castle
berthed. An easy customs check, and we go to a small
cabin, uncomfortably so with a collapsible cot installed.
Some telegrams from Johannesburg are waiting for us. We
will be cooped up here for the next eighteen days, with
smells of decaying fruit and damp ammonia-smelling
diapers. Sailing via St. Helena and Ascension Island to
Tilbury, England.

Port Elizabeth. A liner, pearl-grey hull, entering a
harbour early in the morning. A seaweed covered break-
water, a sludge of fog, a ship sounding its horn, and in the
dampness on the mole fifty Moslems in red fezes standing,
waiting, hardly human, like diver birds grouped on a rock.
Suddenly handkerchiefs appear in their hands and are
limply waved above their heads in silence, still not very
enthusiastic.

The silence and vastness of the liner making its way
slowly into the harbour. Its tiers of deserted decks; chill
of the hour, just before daybreak.

Capetown. The Moslems in full regalia posing, very
patient, for amateur photographers on 'D' Deck in a thin
drizzle of rain. The ship's nurse orders them about. They
are Cape Coloureds, Moslems returning to Capetown after
a nine month trip to Mecca.

Low cloud over the city, Table Mountain invisible;
smoke rising from the business quarters, joined up to low-
hanging discoloured clouds - like a city after a bombard-
ment. The persistent thin rain. Two tugs pulling the
Warwick Castle off its berth. The harbour turns round.
The tugs cast off. Music over the ship's loudspeakers; the
wake stretches out behind. Now we leave this continent;
now the ship sails. Feeling of elation.

...A day out and the Cape rollers begin. Vomit on the
companionway mats, the diningroom half empty, and the
Belgian Congolese children yelling: 'Malade! Malade!'

Two days out and already bored with shipboard life.
St. Helena in the morning. I wrote to Mr. Solomen (or
Solomens) there; his grandfather sold maccaroni to
Napoleon.

St. Helena. Discoloured volcanic cliffs, then the valley,
and Jamestown, with boats coming out. We are to stay
here until evening. I see a high waterfall coming down,
white water, and more boats putting out from the island.
Festive appearance. The islanders come on board to sell
trinkets. I talk to one of the young men. He herds sheep;
he brought some from the back of the island at five this
morning. His sing-song voice. Biblical scene.

The young men are leaving the island, he tells me, to
work on the American air-bases on Ascension. They made
an air-strip along the ridge of a volcanic mountain. They
can double their wages there, working in radio. The jute
factories pay little. Those who stay are attempting to
start a trade union movement - the first in the island's
history. They load jute into the hold. It has a bad smell.
Some of the older islanders are going into domestic
service in Scotland. A butler and housekeeper. He is small,
scorched black by the sun, his sing-song English difficult
to follow.

I go ashore with another passenger - a white-haired,

stout, elderly Chinaman, very polite and formal. Mr. Johns. Very courteous, neatly dressed in a blue suit with a white shirt and dark tie, a raincoat over one arm, a rolled umbrella in his hand (what Chinaman would go without an umbrella?). He carries an expensive attache case, as an emblem of caste? We introduce ourselves. He tells me he was born on St. Helena but left it as a young man to seek his fortune in the USA. He worked for fifty years as a traveller in the Bible trade, married an American lady from Boston, Mass., and is now retired. He is through with the Bible business. He had hoped to spend his last years on the island, but his wife does not care for it - not enough social contact, too many white ants, insufficient refrigeration. They had originally planned to live on the island for three years, in a sort of trial retirement, but no, his wife couldn't stand it; they are leaving again in the spring. He himself would have liked to have stayed, but he would do what his wife wanted; she would never be happy there. They plan to return to Boston.

He introduces me to Pastor Phillips, from Orlando location, Johannesburg, on the steps of Jamestown p.o. I too am from Jo'burg. Orlando!

I make an arrangement to meet Mr. Johns later with Jay (who has stayed on board with the child); we are to take a taxi and visit Longwood House. I take leave of him on a small humpback Chinese bridge, surrounded by white blossoms, with the sound of water trickling in the irrigation streams, no sound of human voices in this quiet backward island retreat a thousand miles from anywhere, and take a walk up the valley - glad to be off the ship.

The Warwick Castle, much diminished, lying offshore about three-quarters of a mile out, seen between two converging cliffs.

Terraces sown with peas and beans, warm dry air, hot sunshine, peace. An outdated greeting to Princess Elizabeth and Prince Philip painted on a hillside. A rustic England of the early nineteenth century perpetuated here. With an annual rainfall of thirty-six inches, a very temperate climate; one could live 1,700 ft. above sea level in a temperature of seventy degrees all the year round.

Longwood House in the afternoon. Napoleon's last resting-place, a long way from the frozen rivers and corpse-strewn plains of the lost Russian campaign. The cold names of the rivers that flow into the Baltic - Vistula, Niemen. Niemen-on-the-ice. Bonaparte getting into a closed carriage with his mameluke at Smorgony, defeated and on his way back to Paris. 'Halted at Jaffa at the western entrance to Asia, and halted at Moscow at the northern gateway to the same continent, he was to go and die among the seas bordering that part of the world where mankind and the sun were born.'

In the billiard-room the pockets are rotting from the table, the green baize turning white with age; the billiard balls in their wooden frames rest behind glass in the hall. Chipped antique objects - the Emperor's cannons.

The smallness of his bed; its green canopy - a child's bed. His death-mask cast in bronze stands on a pedestal. Effigies of him in every room and in the hall. Vain as Voltaire.

St. Helena lies between the two Poles, 'At the extremity of our hemisphere' - says Tacitus - 'one can hear the sound made by the sun sinking into the sea: <u>sonum insuper immergentis audiri.</u>' When Napoleon went out, his spirits low, he passed along stony paths lined with aloes and scented broom.

In the narrow valley known then as Slane or Geranium Valley, and now as Tomb Valley, there is a spring at which Napoleon's Chinese servants, as faithful as Camoëns's Javanese, used to fill their pitchers; weeping willows hang over this spring; green grass, studded with tchampas, grows all around. ('The tchampas,' says the Sanskrit poems, 'for all its colour and perfume, is not a sought-after flower, because it grows on graves.')

Napoleon liked the willows by the spring, but everything saddened him under a sky beneath which life seemed shorter, the sun remaining three days less in that hemisphere than in ours. Towards the end of February 1821, in his sixth year of exile on the rock, he was obliged to take to his bed ('How low I have fallen!.... I have stirred up the whole world, and I cannot lift my eyelids!'), and he did not get up again. He died in Longwood on May 5th, 1821. 'He sleeps like a hermit or a pariah in a valley, at the end of a deserted pathway,' wrote Chateaubriand.

In 1840 the remains were brought home to France - he

had come home to be buried in the grime of Paris.
Bonaparte passed through the tomb, as he passed through
everything, without stopping.

Vague feeling that he did live there once; pined away
and died there; written of by de Seguar, Chateaubriand,
latterly Kafka, fascinated by the horrors of the Russian
campaign. Suffered from migraine, dysyresis (retention
of the urine). Murat, Ney; carnage at Borodino, blood-
soaked fields. He had drilled peep-holes in the window
shutters to spy on the English soldiers going on and off
duty. At daybreak here, forgotten. Never forgotten.

The lazy Azores; three miles of sea below us. The English
clergyman's anaemic full-grown son in the diningroom.
'Oh of course they're not trusworthy as pets.' Finicky
English voice - that strange, slight talk which governed
the British Empire. 'I never take liberties with an
Alsation.' The English ladies opposite us; their
movements, talk, complacency - their security. Lily
Briscoe. Walking on the upper deck. Beginning of an
overcast day. The jet fighter from Ascension, island of
ashes, a pinpoint, then directly over the mast, then four
miles out to sea.

The Canary Islands; Las Palmas. One can smell it approaching; the stench of colonial Spain.

Generalissimo Franco mole. The taxi ride. In the
cathedral the old waxen-faced priest high up in an alcove
reading his office - an image from Goya. The confessional
stained black about the grille: sins (bad breath?) of
generations of humble penitents. An island of bad teeth and
halitosis. Smells of cheap cognac and wine gone sour in the
bars. A vegetable market, white colonnades and green
trellis, all the charm of Spain.

Fish-tinning factories; the Coca-Cola factory under
construction on the hill. An island inundated with
Japanese-made merchandise with falsified US trade marks.
Populated caves in the dirty hills above the town. The well-
dressed tout offering us a Parker pen made in Osaka; another
in the cathedral, shows us the manuscript Vulgate of 1614.

Hot idle days. The tourist class swimming pool with two

feet of water, Belgian Congolese children splashing in it, screaming snipe. Shrouded cars on the fore-deck with Belgium Congo registration plates. Exodus from the troubled Congo.

Circular intimations of calamity. 'The contemporary of Napoleon conceived his completion of European philosophy as the fulfilment of a primary undeveloped origin. The contemporary of Adolf Hitler conceives the identical history of the European spirit as the gradual epiphany of Nihilism.'* So what of Father Adam and his teeming billions of posterity.

The weather turns foul; heavy seas, troughs of grey waves. A port-hole, a stretch of harbour, docks of Las Palmas, a boat loading up alongside the Warwick Castle, a view of burnt hills, already only a memory.

Two port-holes; slothful slop and wallow of the waves striking the side of the ship; grey-green sea agitated all the way to the horizon. Staring before her with empty eyes.

The tarpaulin-shrouded cars on deck. Hardly any place to exercise now. We left Europe four years ago with frightened Germans leaving after the Hungarian uprising; we are going back to Europe with Belgians running from the Belgian Congo.

A dance on the upper deck at night. The engine-driver from Rhodesia, bluff bonhomie. Thrust of the prow. The captain's warm handclasp. Gershwin's <u>Night and Day</u>.

The English Channel.

We reach the mouth of the Thames in the late afternoon, but can't get into Tilbury. There's a dock-strike on (also a printing strike).

When we wake up next morning we're in. Through the port-holes we see English bobbies standing about with their hands behind their backs on the wet dockside. It's raining in grey Tilbury.

*Hans Magnus Enzensberger

SIGNATURE is a new series of shorter works, distinguished by the highly personal and imaginative approach
of the author to his subject. It comprises works of poetry
and prose, fiction and non-fiction, and includes English,
American, and translated texts.